JB HEYDRICH
Ramen, Fred
Reinhard Heydrich: hangman of the third
reich

HOLOCAUST BIOGRAPHIES

Reinhard Heydrich
Hangman of the Third Reich

Fred Ramen

THE ROSEN PUBLISHING GROUP, INC.
NEW YORK

Published in 2001 by The Rosen Publishing Group, Inc.
29 East 21st Street, New York, NY 10010

First Edition

Library of Congress Cataloging-in-Publication Data

Ramen, Fred.
Reinhard Heydrich: hangman of the Third Reich / Fred Ramen.
p. cm. — (Holocaust biographies)
Includes bibliographical references and index.
ISBN 0-8239-3379-2
1. Heydrich, Reinhard, 1904–1942—Juvenile literature. 2.
Nazis—Biography—Juvenile literature. 3. Germany—
History—1933–1945—Juvenile literature. I. Title. II. Series.
DD247.H42 R36 2001
943.086'092—dc21

                                2001002041

Manufactured in the United States of America

Contents

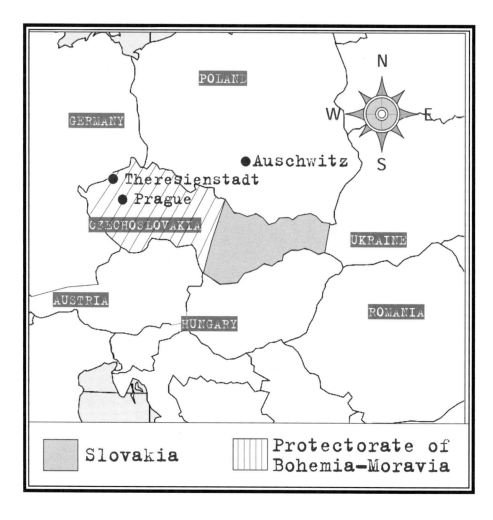

Helpless against the German army, and without the support of either Britain or France, Czechoslovakia was seized by Germany in 1939. After, it was divided into two "nations": the Protectorate of Bohemia-Moravia, which was run by Heydrich and the Third Reich, and Slovakia, a Nazi "puppet state."

Introduction

World War II was nearly three years old in June of 1942, and many throughout Germany had reason to mourn. The conflict with the Soviet Union was beginning to go badly, although it was hoped that the new attacks to capture the city of Stalingrad and the precious oil fields that lay beyond it would at last bring about the collapse of Germany's most dangerous rival. Britain, which had withstood everything the German air force, the *Luftwaffe*, had thrown at it in 1940, was now, in fact, gathering its strength and helping the Americans to drive the Germans and their Italian allies out of North Africa. And, of course, throughout the Third Reich—Nazi Germany—thousands upon thousands lingered painfully in concentration camps. These individuals were being physically and spiritually broken by poor food, savage beatings, and hard labor; not to mention the thousands of Jewish families shipped out of Germany to concentration camps in Poland— camps they would never leave alive.

But it was not for any of these reasons, certainly not on account of the Jews, that Berlin was draped in black on June 9, 1942. Instead, it was for the man who had brought untold suffering to millions of people—the same man who had been involved in some of the worst crimes of the Third Reich, and who had planned and controlled the awful machinery of the Final Solution—the Holocaust—the premeditated murder of six million Jews.

His name was Reinhard Heydrich. He was the number two man in the SS, a possible successor to Adolf Hitler himself, head of the Gestapo (the Third Reich's secret police), and the man in charge of the death camps where the extermination of Europe's Jews was carried out.

Reinhard Heydrich was the man in charge of the death camps where millions of Jews were murdered.

The wake for Heydrich was held in the impressively ugly chancellery building, designed and built by Hitler's personal architect, Albert Speer, who shared with his Führer (Hitler's favorite title for himself, German for "leader") a taste for the grotesquely huge. Hitler himself attended—a rare enough event; since the war had begun, he had shown himself in public less and less often—and was obviously moved and shaken by the death of the man many had thought of as the ideal Nazi. Heydrich, Hitler told one of the dead man's sons, had a heart of iron. There were far too many people who had suffered at the hands of this iron-hearted man, despised outside Germany as "Hangman Heydrich." In Prague, the beautiful capital of Czechoslovakia and the site of Heydrich's final crimes, he was known as "the Butcher of Prague." It was here that he at last had to answer for his crimes, at the hands of an assassin.

Who was this man, unknown to many even inside Germany during his lifetime, and to this day, not nearly as recognizable as the other Nazi leaders such as Hitler or Göring? How had he risen so far in the Nazi government? Why did so many fear him? What was his role in the mass execution of so many people?

And finally, how was he hunted down and murdered, and who was responsible for ending the despicable life of this man?

1. Soldier

Reinhard Tristan Heydrich was born on March 7, 1904, in the central German town of Halle, near Leipzig. His father, Bruno, was an opera singer and composer who was devoted to the music of the great German composer Richard Wagner. He named his sons after characters from two operas: Reinhard, the hero of his own opera, *Amen*; and Tristan, the hero of Wagner's *Tristan und Isolde*.

Raised Under the Shadow of Prejudice

Bruno Heydrich, like many Germans of his day, was extremely patriotic, to the point of being prejudiced against other countries and people who came from them. Germany had only existed as a unified country for thirty-three years when Reinhard was born, and many Germans shared Bruno's fierce devotion to their new empire. Because Germany had become a nation only very recently, it was bent on making itself the equal of the other powerful nations of Europe: France, Russia, and especially Britain.

The struggle to unify Germany had taken most of the nineteenth century and had produced a number of powerful movements and beliefs among many Germans. One was Pan-Germanism, the belief that all of the German-speaking people of Europe (especially those in neighboring Austria-Hungary, ruled by the German-speaking Austrian emperor), should be unified into one German nation (sometimes called Greater Germany). Another was a common belief among Germans that Germany was superior to other nations. Many people who believed this became extremely prejudiced, believing not only that Germany was a superior country, but that Germans were superior to other people, even other races.

Various "scientific" theories were cooked up to support the idea that "Nordic Aryans" (such as the Germans) were racially superior to other people, especially dark-skinned people, who were not even thought to be human beings. People who held these beliefs were often anti-Semitic, or prejudiced against Jewish people, as well—an unfortunate tradition in Germany that went back at least to the Middle Ages. Finally, because it had been Prussia, the part of Germany that had the biggest army and was the least democratic, that finally succeeded in unifying Germany under its king, who became the German emperor, many people in Germany distrusted democracy and loved military glory.

Bruno Heydrich shared all of these beliefs to an extreme degree. He was a German nationalist and a committed anti-Semite. In part, this was because many people in Halle thought that Heydrich, who was Catholic, might have had Jewish ancestry. His mother had remarried after his father died, taking her new husband's name, Suess, which in Germany at the time was thought of as a Jewish name. Her new husband, to the best of anyone's knowledge, was not Jewish, but the rumors that surrounded Bruno kept him from ever being truly accepted by the upper classes of Halle. It is ironic that others who also hated Jews persecuted a man who hated Jews so passionately.

Young Reinhard grew up surrounded by music. His father owned a conservatory, a music school for upper-class children in Halle, and he trained both Reinhard and his little brother Heinz in music. At first, Bruno hoped that Reinhard would become a singer as he had been, but the boy's voice was not good enough. Instead, he was taught how to play the violin. Reinhard eventually became a very good player.

World War I

When Reinhard was ten years old, however, his life and the lives of all Germans were changed forever by the greatest war in history up to that point: World War I.

In Berlin, formerly prosperous Germans protest economic policies in 1927.

The rapid rise of Germany to a world power had caused tension throughout Europe, eventually creating two opposing alliances—the Entente (later called the Allies) of France, Russia and Britain, and the Central Powers of Germany, Austria-Hungary, and Turkey. When the heir to the throne of Austria-Hungary, Archduke Franz Ferdinand, was assassinated in 1914, it sparked a war that would devastate Europe for years.

German strategy called for a quick knockout blow to France that would allow the Germans to turn all their force on Russia, which had a much larger army and population than Germany. In the early days of the war, it seemed like the Germans would succeed against both their enemies; they roared across northern France, driving hard toward Paris, and wrecked two major Russian armies in what is now Poland. But the German attack on France ran out of steam before it could take Paris, and both the Germans and the French (with their British allies) dug in, constructing elaborate networks of trenches that crossed France from the British Channel to the Rhine River. Without tanks or better planes (both eventually developed at the end of the war), the trenches were essentially impossible to capture; this did not, however, prevent both German and French commanders from wasting their men's lives in pointless assaults on the enemy's trenches.

The war dragged on for four years, costing millions of lives. A blockade by the British navy had cut Germany off from the rest of the world; this caused great suffering for the German people, since the nation had to import much of its food. By the end of the war, many people were near starvation.

Bruno Heydrich had brought his sons up to be, if anything, even more blindly pro-German and racist than he was. The Heydriches believed, despite the worsening conditions in Germany, that their side would eventually win. Like many Germans, they felt shocked and betrayed when Germany surrendered on November 11, 1918. How had the best army in the world, which still occupied most of northern France and Belgium, been defeated?

In actuality, by this point, the German army was no longer anything more than a mob. Vital ammunition and supplies were unavailable, and many men would simply fight no longer. The army leadership had been trying to surrender for weeks. It was only when the emperor stepped down and fled to Holland, and a new, democratic government took over, that the final surrender negotiations were able to take place. However, this helped to give rise to the myth of the "stab in the back"—the idea that the civilian government had surrendered when the army still wanted to fight on, "stabbing them in the back."

The situation in Germany was very confusing. Without any preparation, the German people suddenly found themselves in a democracy after many years of nearly absolute rule by the German emperors and Prussian kings. The navy had mutinied in the last days of the war, refusing to take orders and spreading revolution to many of Germany's cities. For a while, it looked as if Germany would undergo a Communist revolution like the one that had started in Russia in 1917. The fate of Central Europe's most powerful nation hung in the balance.

Free Forces

Conservative forces in Germany managed to put down the Communist revolutionaries by organizing their own private armies. These groups, called *Freikorps* (German for "free forces"), mostly composed of army veterans and young men eager for a taste of battle, ruthlessly attacked the revolutionaries. The Freikorps were usually led by people with the worst prejudices of German society, both racist and anti-Semitic; it should come as no surprise that Reinhard Heydrich joined them in 1919, at the age of fifteen, eventually fighting all over central Germany and parts of Poland.

Poland was a new neighbor country of Germany that had been created by the Treaty of Versailles, finally signed in 1919, which ended World War I. New countries, such as Poland, Czechoslovakia, Hungary, and Yugoslavia, were created out of the rubble of the Russian and Austrian-Hungarian Empires.

Freikorps fighters, with swastikas emblazoned on their helmets, sweep through the streets of Berlin looking for people to attack.

Because these countries had been the victims of repression under the Russians and Austrians, their people were happy to finally have their independence. But for Germans, the Treaty of Versailles was a cruel blow.

The treaty stripped Germany of its overseas colonies. It gave parts of Germany to the new nation of Poland. The German territory between France and the Rhine River—the Rhineland—was demilitarized; in other words, the Germans could not place troops there to defend their borders. The German army itself was reduced to a 100,000-man defense force, and the Germans were forbidden to build submarines or maintain an air force. Germany and all her people were forced to accept blame for having started the war; to make amends for this, huge reparations—payments to the Allies for having started the war—were ordered, which proved to be a crushing burden for the German economy. Germany was humiliated and destroyed as a powerful nation.

All of this was very difficult for many Germans to accept, especially people who shared the views of Bruno Hcydrich and his sons. The defeat in the war had been bitter enough; the Treaty of Versailles was more than many could bear, and it strengthened the feeling that Germany had been betrayed by its government. Meanwhile, the bottom had fallen out of the German economy, ruining many people, including Heydrich's father. Unemployment rose, and inflation made the money people did have almost worthless. Clearly, the musical career his father wanted for Reinhard was out of the question.

Reinhard had a solution, however: He would join the navy.

2. Sailor

That the son of a musical family, fiercely conservative and nationalistic and familiar with the rough-and-tumble life of the *Freikorps*, should choose to join the navy is not as odd as it sounds. The German navy in the 1920s remained, in many ways, the pride of what was left of the German military.

The Seeds of German Nationalism

One of the goals of the German Empire in the early part of the twentieth century had been to build a navy that would be a match for Britain's Royal Navy and serve as a symbol of Germany's new supremacy in both Europe and

the world. Immense sums of money, both from
the government and from private citizens,
were poured into the project of creating the
most technically advanced navy in the world.
During World War I, however, the German navy
had been unable to break the British blockade
of Germany; its pride was further damaged by
the series of mutinies onboard navy ships that
started a revolution in 1918. After the war, the
remnants of the German High Seas Fleet, the
best ships in the navy, had been rounded up
and anchored under the watchful eyes of the
Royal Navy at their base in Scapa Flow, off the
Scottish coast. There, on January 31, 1920, the
German crews had sunk their own ships, a
desperate act of defiance that earned them a
hero's welcome in Germany.

Although the Versailles Treaty restricted its
size, the navy's commander, Admiral Erich
Raeder, was determined to create a force that
would not only be rebuilt to challenge the
Royal Navy, but one that would represent the
best of the German armed forces. Politically

conservative, Raeder wanted the officers of the German navy to reflect his own personal views; to be morally upright and superbly capable of doing their jobs. Raeder and many of his officers had little respect for the new German government, the Weimar Republic (so-called because the city of Weimar in central Germany was where its constitution had been written). Many of the officers in the navy, like Heydrich, had served in the *Freikorps* fighting against the forces of the government they were now supposed to protect.

Heydrich, the Loner

Heydrich, very tall and somewhat awkward at this age, had trouble fitting in at first. Although his pale, angular features and blond hair seemed the very embodiment of the Aryan ideal, the rumors about his family being Jewish followed him to the naval academy at Kiel, in northern Germany, and he was insulted and shunned by the other cadets. In response, he concentrated on his studies, keeping away from his fellow students and earning a reputation as a loner. He studied English, French, and Russian, so he would be able to understand the activities of the countries he considered the enemy; he also became an expert radio technician. He was an excellent athlete, enjoying swimming, small-boat sailing, horseback riding, and especially fencing. He also liked to play his violin alone in empty parts of the ships he sailed on, and he read spy, thriller, and detective novels in his spare time.

Heydrich was very unpopular with the sailors he commanded; they found him to be a cruel person who drove them hard and punished them for the slightest offense. However, he made an important friend during his days in the navy: Wilhelm Canaris, who would later be an admiral and the head of German military intelligence. Like Heydrich, Canaris was a conservative with no

respect for the Weimar government. Heydrich
became friendly with Canaris and his wife,
who played the cello, and would often visit
their house to play duets.

Heydrich had joined the navy in the
spring of 1922. Although the German
economy was beginning to recover from the
devastation of the war, within a year it would
be threatened again with political turmoil
that made famous the man who was soon to
control the destiny of Germany: Adolf Hitler.

Hitler's Dream for the Nazi Party

Hitler had been born in the city of Linz,
which was then part of Austria-Hungary, in
1889. As a young man, he had attempted to
start a career as an artist, even traveling to
Vienna, the capital of Austria, to attend art
school. He was unable to get into school,
however, and had to make do by painting
picture postcards for tourists.

When World War I broke out, Hitler joined the German army; he served as a message-runner on the western front, relaying orders from headquarters to the soldiers in the trenches. He often came under enemy fire, and was twice decorated for his bravery.

Hitler was incredibly bitter about the way the war had ended. He believed in the "stab in the back" theory, and was a harsh critic of the Weimar Republic. While investigating anti-government groups for the army after the war, he attended a meeting of the German Workers' Party, which he joined after giving a fiery speech that attacked the government. He quickly moved to take over the party, which he renamed the National Socialist German Workers' Party (known by its German initials, NSDAP)—the Nazis.

Hitler proved himself to not only be a brilliant speaker, but a tireless organizer. He created a special wing of the party, the *Sturmabteilung* (SA), or Stormtroopers (also known as Brownshirts because of the color of

Hitler leads a Sturmabteilung unit in an NSDAP parade in Weimar. The sign at right reads "Germany, wake up!"

their uniforms; the name means "protective squad"). The SA was made up of army veterans and common thugs whose job was literally to beat up the opposition. Membership in the party grew, and he attracted some prominent Germans, including the flying ace Hermann Göring, who became head of the SA.

By 1923, Hitler decided the time had come to lead a National Socialist revolution against the Weimar Republic. His plan was to surround a beer hall in Munich, the southern German city that was the capital of the state of Bavaria, while the heads of the Bavarian government were there attending a rally. He would order them to hand the government over to him; then he would lead his followers on a march to Berlin, the German capital, overthrow the Weimar government, and create

A large crowd gathers in Munich to hear Nazi leaders speak during the Beer Hall Putsch.

the dictatorship that he felt was necessary to make Germany a world power again.

His plan started well: He captured the heads of the Bavarian government at the beer hall. But after that everything went wrong. His prisoners managed to slip away in the night, and called out the police and army. The next day, Hitler and the Nazis attempted to march into the center of Munich, believing that the police would never fire on German citizens. They were wrong. Sixteen Nazis were killed, and many others were wounded. Hitler fled unharmed from the "battle," but soon was captured and put on trial for treason. He was convicted, but only sentenced to five years in prison; he ended up serving only nine months of this sentence, using the time to record his racist and anti-Semitic beliefs in his book *Mein Kampf* (My Struggle).

After his release from prison, Hitler came up with a new strategy: He would take over Germany from inside, using the democratic process to get the Nazis elected to power, and then he would take over and make himself dictator.

Reinhard Heydrich naturally supported Hitler's movement, though as a naval officer he did nothing publicly to help the Nazis. However, his politics may have played a role in the most humiliating experience of his life.

The Rise and Fall of Navy Life

Heydrich had begun a very promising career in the navy. His technical expertise with radios, his knowledge of several foreign languages, and his athletic ability made him the very picture of an ideal navy officer. In 1928, he was assigned to shore duty in Kiel. Officially, he was a communications officer; unofficially, he may have been involved in spying, listening in on the radio communications of other nations and helping to break their codes. It is certain that he was well regarded by many officers at high levels of the German navy.

No longer the awkward eighteen-year-old he had been when he first entered the navy, Heydrich was now a tall, muscular, handsome man, whose only noteworthy physical characteristics were a broken nose (the result of two horseback-riding accidents), and a rather high-pitched voice. Heydrich, however, was apparently very attractive to women; unfortunately, he became a notorious womanizer who went from affair to affair with little regard for the feelings of the girls he was seeing. This got him into serious trouble in 1931.

In December of 1930, Heydrich met Lina von Osten, the daughter of a schoolmaster with noble ancestry. Just two days after the meeting, they became engaged. Lina, tall and blonde herself, shared not only Heydrich's Nordic looks, but his politics as well; she and her family were well-known Nazis.

However, at the beginning of the new year, 1931, Heydrich found himself in a fight for his naval career. Another girl that he had known claimed that her honor had been violated. She made this claim because after Heydrich met her at a dance, he spent the night in her room, which was a serious breach of etiquette for a naval officer at that time. The girl's father demanded that Heydrich marry her. Heydrich refused to do so, with an attitude so arrogant that the court of honor appointed to investigate the charge

Reinhard Heydrich attends a concert in Prague with his wife Lina on the eve of his assassination.

decided to dismiss him from the navy. His appeals failed to change this decision, and Reinhard Heydrich found himself an unwilling civilian.

It is unknown how much Heydrich's political beliefs affected the navy's decision. Later, when he had begun to rise through the Nazi Party ranks, he told people that his sympathy for the party had angered some of his superiors, who had conspired to bring charges against him. Certainly his political beliefs angered some members of the navy just as much as his shocking conduct with women; but whether or not this was the primary reason he was kicked out of the navy will never be known.

He could not have chosen a worse time to be unemployed. The German economic recovery had been wiped out by the crash of the New York stock market in 1929, which triggered a worldwide depression. Unemployment soared in Germany, and inflation made many people's money worthless. It took millions of deutschmarks (the Germany currency) just to buy bread.

Lina remained engaged to Heydrich, but he could not marry her without first getting a job. Finding the idea of working in most civilian businesses distasteful, but unable to get work at sea, Heydrich cast about to find a job that would remind him of his days as a military officer.

He was soon to find just the sort of thing he had been looking for, a job that would lift him to undreamed-of heights of power and eventually make him one of the two or three most powerful men in Germany. He would join the Nazi Party.

3. Spy

Hitler and the Nazis had made important strides by the time Heydrich joined the party in June of 1931. Elections had constantly added to the number of Nazis at all levels of government, and important connections were being created between the Nazi leaders and the heads of Germany's largest corporations. The bad economy actually helped the Nazis, because it increased the public's unhappiness with the Weimar government.

The SS, Nazi Elite

Heydrich started out as a member of the SA, or the Stormtroopers, who had earned a bad reputation. But he already had set his sights on joining another organization within the Nazi Party: the *Schutzstaffel,* or SS.

Originally created to be Hitler's guard unit under the leadership of Heinrich Himmler, a chicken farmer four years older than Heydrich, the SS was rapidly being transformed into the elite of the Nazi Party, whose members had to have absolutely pure German blood.

Hitler approved of Himmler's expansion of SS power, as he felt it would help him control

Heydrich works at his desk, outlining Hitler's plans for the murder of Europe's Jews.

the other Nazi leaders, especially Ernst Röhm, the head of the SA. The SS had a responsibility to watch over the rest of the party and keep records of the activities of all its members, as well as the activities of groups who opposed the Nazis. Himmler, whose round, pudgy face and comical eyeglasses hid an iron will and ruthless determination to get his own way, was a remarkable administrator, but he had no experience in running a spy operation. He needed someone with the appropriate background to take over that aspect of SS operations. On the advice of a friend who was a high-ranking member of the SS, he turned to Heydrich.

He had made an inspired choice. Heydrich had a very impressive memory, which allowed him to coordinate the information his agents brought him. He also proved to be an excellent administrator who organized his new department, the *Sicherheitsdienst* (Security Service) or SD, into a powerful, efficient force. From its origins as a small group of men operating out of Munich, it would become one of the most feared organizations in the world.

Germany's New Leader

The change would begin on January 20, 1933. On that day, President Paul von Hindenburg, under pressure from conservative groups in the Reichstag, Germany's parliament (roughly the equivalent of the U.S. Congress), appointed Adolf Hitler to be chancellor of Germany. This had been made possible only through Hitler's plan of working within the system, gathering his strength until the Nazis were the largest party in Germany. His conservative allies in the Reichstag, who had hoped to control him once he was in charge, were soon disappointed; Hitler moved quickly to grab absolute power.

One of the means Hitler used to seize that power was the Enabling Act, which gave him dictatorial leadership. Many events in Nazi Germany were staged; in order to convince the people to support one of Hitler's power grabs, an appropriate "crisis" had to be created. In this case, it was the destruction of the Reichstag building in Berlin, which burned on February 27, 1933. At the time, the fire was blamed on the Communists, and used to justify granting Hitler dictatorial powers. In actuality, however, it is thought that Nazi agents set the fire; these men were probably under the direction of Reinhard Heydrich, who was gaining a reputation as the man to turn to for undercover operations.

Heydrich was sent outside of Germany several months later to attend a disarmament conference being held in Geneva, Switzerland. His obnoxious attitude offended many of the participants, and his one notable accomplishment was flying the swastika flag (the symbol of the Nazi party; it had not yet become the national flag of Germany) over the hotel in which he was staying.

Soon, however, Heydrich was back in Germany, and working hard at building up the SD as well as expanding his other powers. He and Himmler created a new secret police organization in Bavaria, bypassing the existing police forces there. These two men, experts at playing the game of Nazi politics, found new ways to tighten their iron grip on the German people.

Opposition to the Stormtroopers

By 1934, the SA had become a major headache for Hitler and the other Nazi leaders. The largest wing of the party, with some two million members, the Brownshirts were also dangerous: They were the equivalent of deputy police officers in Prussia, Germany's largest state, and many members had guns or other weapons. Their leader, Ernst Röhm, wanted to make the SA the most important section of the Nazi Party, and even moved to bring the army under his leadership. The generals in charge of the army, many of whom were members of the

The Brownshirts pictured here were part of a force of two million men, mostly untrained criminals.

older Prussian aristocracy and looked down on Hitler and the Nazis, were opposed to this move. The SA was composed of criminals, without military training or discipline. Furthermore, Röhm was a homosexual, and this offended the army leadership.

Hitler had problems with the SA as well. The leaders of the Prussian wing of the Brownshirts, Otto and Gregor Strasser, wanted to have a "second revolution" that would toss out the existing power structure of Germany and replace it with an SA organization. Such a move would have been fought by both the army and the upper classes of Germany, and would probably have destroyed the Nazi Party.

Hermann Göring—who was the minister of the interior of Prussia, which gave him control over that state's police forces—was also opposed to the SA, mainly because he wanted the support of the army generals so that he could become minister of war. He therefore found himself a reluctant ally of Himmler and Heydrich, who wanted to wipe out the SA , making the SS the most important wing of the Nazi Party.

The Night of the Long Knives

In 1934, Göring turned over control of his own secret police force, the Gestapo (*Geheime*

Staatspolizei, or secret state police) to the SS, which made it the secret police of all Germany and a symbol of terror throughout Europe. In return, Göring expected help in his fight against the SA, and Heydrich gave him exactly what he was looking for.

Working carefully behind the scenes, Heydrich created evidence that the SA and their leaders were planning a rebellion against Hitler; whether this was to convince Hitler to let the SS act against the SA, or whether Hitler himself was behind the plot from the beginning, is not known with certainty.

What *is* known is that on the night of June 30, 1934, while the leaders of the SA were gathered together, the SS went into motion. Röhm and most of the other leaders were arrested and shot by the SS. Other opponents of the Nazis were rounded up as well, and put into concentration camps or killed. For months afterward, bodies were discovered in out-of-the-way locations throughout Germany. This brutal purge, the Night of the

Long Knives, as it came to be known, was
directed by Himmler and Heydrich, and
made possible only by Heydrich's careful
work with the SD and the Gestapo. When the
dust had settled, Hitler had disbanded the
SA, put the SS in charge of the concentration
camps, and made the SD the Nazi Party's
only spy service.

Reinhard Heydrich (far right) and Heinrich
Himmler (left, standing) are on the way to a
political rally.

Spy

For years, Heydrich continued to track the SA leaders who had escaped, most notably Otto Strasser, who had managed to go into exile in Czechoslovakia. There he founded an anti-Nazi group, the Black Front, which broadcast anti-Nazi messages over the border into Germany. In 1935 Heydrich decided to kidnap Strasser's radio engineer, Rudolf Formis, and set up an elaborate plan using a female agent to lure Formis to a spot where he could be kidnapped.

Unfortunately, not only did Formis suspect what was going on, the agent in charge of the operation, Alfred Naujocks, had few of the qualities that one would want in a spy, preferring to use violence rather than thoughtfulness to solve problems. He got into a gunfight with Formis that left the engineer dead; while the transmitter was destroyed, the Black Front soon had it running again, and the Nazis lost a valuable propaganda opportunity—having Formis "confess" to his "crimes" (after being tortured).

Nazi Propaganda Continues

In August of 1936, Berlin was the host of the Olympic Games. Heydrich was given the responsibility of coordinating the propaganda for the games; his job was to cover up the true face of Nazi Germany, and instead present an image of a happy, peaceful, and productive nation whose progress the entire world should envy.

Heydrich used a variety of schemes to pull off this massive cover-up. First, he had all racist and anti-Semitic posters and banners removed from Berlin before the international press and the world's athletes arrived. Attacks and assaults on the Jews, which had been steadily increasing since Hitler took power, were also halted. Next, Heydrich orchestrated a variety of carefully planned events for Berlin's guests. To give the best possible impression to the reporters covering the Olympics, he proposed they visit factories, public buildings, and the ordinary homes of

Adolf Hitler rides in a motorcade through the
Brandenburg Gate to the opening ceremonies of the
eleventh Olympiad in Berlin on August 1, 1936.

German citizens. Wherever they went, the smiling girls and boys of the Hitler Youth met them, singing patriotic songs and presenting their guests with flowers.

This deception practiced by the Nazis went so far as to allow some Jewish athletes—fencer Helene Meyer and hockey player Rudi Ball—to play on their teams. In this way, the Nazis could lie about the discrimination and violence that were being directed at the Jews in Germany.

Although the Germans did very well at the Olympics, winning thirty-three gold medals, their well-planned celebration of Aryan supremacy failed at one key point. African American track star Jesse Owens won four gold medals, setting or tying four world records and demonstrating that the Nazi theories of racial differences were nothing more than unscientific prejudice. Still, although many were not fooled by Heydrich's lies, other people who only saw movies or read articles about the Olympics did not understand how cruel and racist the Nazi regime was actually becoming.

Heydrich and Himmler had now made the SS the most powerful wing of the Nazi Party. However, just as Hitler was not satisfied with total power in Germany and lusted after the mastery of Europe and the world, Himmler and his able deputy wanted to extend their power throughout every part of German life. Himmler dreamed of an SS nation, a Germany where the Aryan aristocracy that made up the SS would be the lords of the earth, and the lesser races (the Slavs, for example) would exist merely to serve their permanent masters.

In the next few years, as Europe tumbled into the most catastrophic war in human history, Heydrich would help his friend and superior come close to achieving this horrific vision. Within a short time, the SS would be master of Germany, and Germany would be the master of most of Europe.

4. Warrior

While Heydrich and Himmler dreamed of an empire within the Nazi Party, Hitler dreamed of an empire in Europe. Between 1936 and 1939, he took the steps necessary to make his dream a reality.

Hitler's Vision of a Greater Germany

Hitler's vision of the future of Germany had three key parts. First, it would be necessary to create a "Greater Germany" consisting of all the German-speaking parts of Europe. Basically, this meant Austria, but included parts of Czechoslovakia and the areas of Poland that had once been part of Germany, as well as areas with a Nordic or "Aryan" heritage such as Denmark, and possibly Norway and Sweden.

The second part of his plan was to secure *Lebensraum* (German for "living space") in eastern Europe and, especially, the Soviet Union. As had been made painfully clear by World War I, Germany was not self-sufficient in many necessary items such as oil, metals such as tungsten, and food. By conquering the lands to the east, Germany could assure itself a generous supply of all these resources and, most importantly, the supply could not be blocked by a naval blockade such as the one the British had established during World War I.

The final piece of Hitler's vision was the elimination of Jews from Germany and those parts of Europe that he was going to dominate. During the early years of the Third Reich, this was accomplished mainly by forcing Jewish people to emigrate, or leave, Germany; but Hitler had always meant to exterminate, once and for all, every Jew he could place under his power. He never lost sight of this goal.

Violating the Treaty of Versailles

In order to complete his plan successfully, however, Hitler needed to solve a number of problems. The German economy had to improve. He had to rebuild the army and navy, and recreate a new air force. This would require not only the complete loyalty of the army generals (which he could not yet be sure of), but also breaking the restrictions of the Versailles treaty.

Hitler had already begun secretly rearming Germany, increasing the size of its army and making Göring the head of an "aviation club" that would eventually become the feared *Luftwaffe*, the new German air force. In 1936, Hitler took yet another step that was designed to not only strike at the Versailles treaty, but increase the army's loyalty to his leadership.

Since 1919, Germany had been forbidden by the terms of the treaty to place troops in the Rhineland, the territory between the

Hitler addresses the Reichstag at Berlin's Kroll Opera House in 1939.

Rhine River and the French border. Now Hitler ordered the army to once again occupy this area. It was a risky move; the French and British, with much larger armies, could easily have swept away the tiny German forces. But neither one took any action; fear of starting a new war and a belief that the terms of the Versailles treaty had been too harsh to begin with seem to have held them back. Hitler's

bold move won him the approval not only of
the German people, but his own generals,
who had feared provoking the British and the
French. It was not to be the first time that
Hitler had judged the situation better than
his generals.

Over the next few years, Hitler continued
to openly defy the Versailles treaty. The army
had increased in size far beyond the 100,000
men the treaty had held it to, the navy began
building battleships and submarines, and the
Luftwaffe, the pride of the new military, was
made into a formidable weapon.

Hitler and Heydrich Take Germany's War Ministry

Yet Hitler still faced opposition from two
members of his military staff: General Werner
von Blomberg, the minister of war, and
General Werner von Fritsch, head of the army
and a critic of the increasing power that the
SS wielded in German society. Himmler and

Heydrich turned their attention to these two men, hoping to discredit them.

Their first target was von Fritsch. Because the general was not married, they tried to compile evidence that he was a homosexual, a charge that would have caused the army to dismiss him. But Hitler, who refused to allow an SS crackdown on the army, blocked Himmler and Heydrich in this attempt because, even at this point, the army had enough power to overthrow Hitler and the rest of the Nazis. Heydrich, however, with his usual efficiency, kept all the "evidence" he had accumulated on the general, waiting for a better time to strike.

This opportunity came in 1938, when a scandal brought down the war minister, von Blomberg. He had married a young girl in January of that year, and within a few weeks, rumors began to circulate about his new wife. The Gestapo claimed to have obscene pictures of the girl, whose mother had run a rather shady massage parlor in Berlin.

(Technicians in the Gestapo photo labs most likely altered these photos.) In any case, Göring, who still wanted von Blomberg's job, took the pictures to Hitler, seizing the moment. Heydrich and Himmler also brought Hitler "evidence" that von Fritsch was a homosexual, further demonstrating the "corruption" of the army officers. Both von Blomberg and von Fritsch were forced to resign; although a court of honor eventually found von Fritsch not guilty, he did not get his job as army commander back. Instead, Hitler took over the War Ministry and made himself head of the army.

Hitler took care to place officers most loyal to him in charge of the army's day-to-day operations. Furthermore, he had made it clear what would happen to generals who dared oppose him. Von Fritsch eventually returned to duty and was killed by a sniper during the invasion of Poland; he was probably looking to die a soldier's death rather than be murdered by the Nazis.

Hitler's Power Grows

Hitler had further consolidated his power by violating the Treaty of Versailles yet again in 1938: He brought about the *Anschluss*, the union of Germany and Austria specifically forbidden by the treaty. As was usual with the Nazis' outrages, an "excuse" had to be found for this move; in this case, agitation by Austrian Nazis resulted in the German army being "invited" to enter Austria to restore order. Shortly thereafter, a vote was taken by the Austrians (carefully monitored by Heydrich's Gestapo) that formally integrated the two countries. Again, the Western Allies, Britain and France, stood by and did nothing.

Now Hitler moved to seize another country, a move that would have fateful complications for him, Germany, and Heydrich: He attempted to take over Czechoslovakia.

This beautiful country had been formed out of parts of Austria-Hungary at the end of World

War I, and had accomplished much in its short lifetime. It had an excellent army, was protected by strong forts along its border with Germany, and had thriving industries. But, it also had a fatal weakness: a large German population, concentrated along the German border in a region known as the Sudetenland.

Because of his desire to create a Greater Germany, as well as the strategic importance of Czechoslovakia (its Bohemia and Moravia regions had vital deposits of iron and coal, as well as excellent weapons factories), Hitler had encouraged the creation of pro-Nazi groups in the Sudetenland. Heydrich had close relations with the leader of one of these groups: Karl Hermann Frank, a brutal man who wanted nothing less than the destruction of the Czech nation.

Seizing Czechoslovakia

Under the guidance of the Germans, the Sudeten Nazis began to stir up trouble for the

Karl Hermann Frank, state secretary of the
Protectorate of Bohemia-Moravia, with Heydrich.

Czechoslovak nation. Hitler made increasingly
loud demands that the (nonexistent)
persecutions of these Germans cease, and that
the Sudetenland be added to the rest of
Germany. The Czechs, under their president,
Edvard Benes (one of the leaders of the
original independence movement that had
fought against the Austrians before World War
I) opposed this move, as it would mean giving

up the line of excellent forts that protected their border with the Germans. Hitler persisted, however, and told his generals to prepare to go to war with the Czech nation. Because Czechoslovakia had made an alliance with both France and the Soviet Union, this could have provoked another European war; but Hitler didn't care, nor did he listen to his generals, who were not at all confident that the still-rebuilding German army was ready to dominate the Czech border.

At the last moment, war was averted. Members of the four great powers of western Europe—France, Britain, Germany, and Germany's ally, Italy, which had its own dictator, Benito Mussolini, met in Munich. The Czechs were not invited to the discussions. The British prime minister, Neville Chamberlain, got all parties to agree to allow the Germans to take the Sudetenland; in return, Hitler promised that he did not want any other territory in Europe. It was a cruel blow to Czechoslovakia, which, without its

The historic 1938 meeting in Munich between (left to right) British prime minister Neville Chamberlain, Adolf Hitler, and French premier Edouard Daladier.

forts or the support of the British and French, would be helpless against the Germans. Under German pressure, Benes resigned and went into exile in London. Within a year, the Germans seized the rest of Czechoslovakia, which they broke into two "nations," the Protectorate of Bohemia-Moravia, which was run directly by the Third Reich, and Slovakia, which was supposed to be an independent country, but was actually a Nazi "puppet state." The Gestapo was given full power to round up dissidents and opponents of the Nazis, and thousands of arrests were made.

The failure of diplomacy to stop Hitler had now been made perfectly clear, and Britain and France made the decision to oppose Hitler's next demands. This did not give the Führer any cause for delay; instead, he prepared for his next territorial grab, this time involving Poland. Two steps were necessary: He had to form a pact with the Soviets and he needed an excuse to invade Poland.

The Invasion of Poland

The first step was an agreement with the Soviet Union. Although he had been a committed foe of Communism ever since his days in the army, Hitler realized that the Soviets would likely oppose an invasion of neighboring Poland. So, in an about-face, he negotiated a nonaggression pact with the

Soviets in the summer of 1939. Secretly, he also made plans with Joseph Stalin, the Soviet dictator, to divide Poland between the two of them after the German invasion.

The next step that was required was an excuse to invade Poland. Once again, Hitler turned to Heydrich, who was soon to be given control over all of Germany's police forces—the Gestapo, SD, and the civilian police—all of which were to be combined in a single office called the RSHA, or Reich Security Main Office. Heydrich quickly developed a secret plan, code-named "Operation Tannenberg" after the tremendous battle won by the Germans against the Russians in Poland during the opening days of World War I.

Operation Tannenberg was designed to be an attack on a German radio station in Gleiwitz, near the Polish border. The attackers, however, would not be Poles but SS men, disguised in Polish uniforms and led by Alfred Naujocks. To add to the deception, several bodies would be left scattered about, also wearing Polish uniforms—evidence of how the "invaders" had been beaten back. These would not be the bodies of Polish soldiers, either, but those of prisoners from a German concentration camp who would be killed at the site; they were called "canned goods" in the secret communications about the plan. Naujocks, however, proved as inept in the "attack" on Gleiwitz as he had four years

Heydrich (standing, left) meets with Himmler (seated, right) and other SS officers in 1938.

earlier in Czechoslovakia. The plan was to interrupt the main German radio program and issue a message in Polish and German, proclaiming the attack and claiming Polish responsibility. Unfortunately, none of his agents could figure out how to relay their signal to the German radio network, so this part of the plan was abandoned. Naujocks instead contented himself with planting the "canned goods," which did a poor job of fooling anyone, as they had all been shot in the head at close range. However, it was enough for Hitler. On September 1, 1939, the day after the "attack," German tanks and planes were sweeping across the Polish border. Flying one of the fighters was Heydrich himself, who had learned how to be a pilot over the previous few years.

Two days later, Britain and France kept their word to their Polish allies and declared war on Germany. World War II had begun.

5. Butcher

As in the case of Czechoslovakia, Hitler's generals were reluctant to start an assault on Poland that could result in another world war. They were all too aware that Germany was not yet ready to fight a major conflict. But Hitler was convinced that they could avoid a lengthy fight with the new technique of blitzkrieg, a German word meaning "lightning war."

Blitzkrieg used close cooperation between planes and tanks to allow for rapid attacks. Unlike what happened in World War I, the enemy would be given no time to dig in; instead, the tanks would use their speed and power to batter down all resistance. Blitzkrieg was a total success against the undermanned

Polish army, which had far fewer tanks than the Germans and in some places still used cavalry—soldiers on horseback—to fight the Germans. By September 17, the fighting was effectively over, and Poland, divided between the Nazis and the Soviets, had ceased to exist.

Heydrich's SS Mission

Right behind the advancing units of the German army came the SS, who had been given a mission by Hitler to destroy the Polish ruling class and make the rest of the population slaves to the Reich. It was Heydrich's security police that carried out this assignment, especially the notorious *Einsatzkommando,* the "special action" commandos, who were given the job of killing the enemies of the Nazis. "Special action" was a rather grim SS joke; such crimes as murder, torture, and, eventually, genocide—the killing of an entire group of people—were all referred to as "special" treatment.

The Jews were not to be spared special treatment. The first step was the eviction of Jewish people from the various regions of Poland. These Jews were then ruled by Germany's central government agencies, the Nazi puppet state in Poland.

This was one more step in the Nazi's long history of brutality toward Jews. Even before Hitler had come to power, the Nazis had led

By January 1945, about 40,000 Germans served in SS units, spreading terror throughout Europe.

boycotts of Jewish-owned businesses, and Jews were frequent targets of attacks by the SA.

In 1935, a series of laws known as the Nuremburg Laws were passed. These stripped Jewish Germans of their citizenry, forbade marriages between Jews and non-Jews, and generally made life extremely difficult for Germany's Jews. It should be noted that the Nazi definition of Jewishness was a racial one; it did not matter what religion a person actually belonged to—if he or she had Jewish ancestors, the Nazis considered him or her a Jew and acted accordingly.

The Night of Broken Glass

The most horrific example of Nazi brutality against the Jews before World War II was the series of riots and attacks known as *Kristallnacht*, or the "Night of Broken Glass." On the night of November 9–10, 1938, the Nazis led a series of attacks on synagogues and

Jewish businesses throughout Germany.
Millions of dollars in damage was done,
destroying nearly every synagogue in
Germany. Many Jews were killed or injured,
and thousands more ended up in
concentration camps. Behind the scenes,
Heydrich coordinated much of this mayhem,
giving instructions on where to attack, and
when to use fire to destroy synagogues and
when to just smash them (to avoid setting
other buildings on fire). He also used his total
control over Germany's police forces to
prevent the arrest of the Nazi thugs who
were doing all the damage.

After the Nazis achieved the goal of
Lebensraum in the east, the Jews of Germany
began to be evicted into Poland, where
the *Einsatzgruppen* (squadrons of the
Einsatzkommando) would be able to prey upon
them. However, Hitler and Heydrich were not
yet satisfied with this program, and would soon
face even greater difficulties in achieving their
goal of the destruction of Europe's Jews.

Local residents watch as a synagogue burns in
Opava, Germany, during *Kristallnacht*.

France Surrenders

The year 1940 was a busy one for Heydrich. During the winter, he once again was flying a fighter plane as a combat pilot, this time over Norway, which the Germans had recently invaded. His flying activities may also have been a cover for the setting up of Gestapo and SS units to wipe out the tenacious Norwegian resistance movement. But soon Heydrich was back in Germany, helping Hitler plan his next bold stroke: the conquest of France.

Although Germany, France, and Britain had been at war since September of 1939, little had happened on the western front. Most of the German army was fighting in Poland. The French were content to crouch behind the Maginot Line (a series of forts that lined their border with Germany, but not their border with Belgium), the location of the massive German invasion of 1914 that had come close to knocking the French out of that war within a month. The British called this phase of the conflict the "Phony War"; the Germans called it the *Sitzkrieg* or "Sitting War."

These French fortifications were too strong to assault from the front, but Hitler had a bold plan. Once again, the Germans would try to invade France from the north, swinging through neutral Belgium and Holland. As they did so, the French and British would move into those countries to defend them. Then, the rest of the German army would sweep through the rocky and forested region known as the Ardennes, which was not protected by the Maginot Line because the French did not believe tanks could drive through it. Heydrich's role in all of this was to use his spy service to mislead the Allies as to where the attack would come; he did this superbly, and they fell right into Hitler's trap. The British and French were surrounded in Belgium, and only the heroic work of the Royal Navy, which managed to float some 300,000 French and British soldiers to safety in England, saved the Allies from total defeat. The Germans then swept through France, which surrendered on June 22, 1940.

Operation Barbarossa and the Eastern Front

Only Britain held out now against the Germans; Hitler expected that they would come to terms with him very soon. But the British were stubborn and refused to end the war. To bring them to their knees, Hitler unleashed the *Luftwaffe*, which began a series of bombing raids and fighter attacks known as the Battle of Britain. Once more, Heydrich was in the air during this desperate struggle. But the German actions were not enough; by the end of the year, it was clear that Britain would not surrender anytime soon.

Frustrated, Hitler returned to his grand vision of *Lebensraum*. Convincing himself that the British were only holding out because they believed that the Soviets would one day turn on the Germans, he began preparations for a massive assault called Operation Barbarossa that would overwhelm the Soviets through the power of blitzkrieg.

The invasion, which began in June of 1941, caught the Soviets by surprise, and the Germans rapidly advanced towards Moscow, the Soviet capital. (This invasion also saw the end of Heydrich's career as a pilot; shot down by the Soviets, he was forbidden to fly again by Himmler.) However, as summer turned to autumn and then to winter, the invasion slowed. The muddy Russian autumn bogged the tanks down, and then the vicious Russian winter froze them in their tracks. Many of the German soldiers were still in their summer uniforms and suffered greatly from the cold, snow, and wind.

For the SS, the success of the German armies in 1940 and 1941 meant that now most of the Jews of Europe were either in Nazi-controlled or Nazi-allied countries. At first, the *Einsatzgruppen* had been sent into the former Soviet areas, where they killed not only Jews, but

Soviet prisoners of war, especially the political officers called "commissars" whose job it was to make sure that the Soviet army remained loyal to Communism. As the Einsatzgruppen went about their work on the eastern front, there were horrible scenes of mass slaughter, of people forced to dig ditches and then marched into them to be shot with machine guns.

Heydrich's Final Solution

Even the hardened men of the SS found it difficult to kill at the rate that Hitler and Heydrich desired. Experiments were made with vans modified so that their exhaust fumes ran directly into a sealed passenger compartment, poisoning its occupants. Soon, a decision was made to continue this method of killing on a much larger scale.

On January 20, 1942, at the request of Göring, Heydrich held a meeting in the Berlin suburb of Wannsee with the heads of the SS

Nazi officials planned the Final Solution at the Wannsee Conference, held in this building.

from the various conquered regions of Europe; this Wannsee Conference addressed the Final Solution of the "Jewish question." Heydrich's plan was to bring all the Jews of Europe into Poland, where they would be put to work for the Third Reich. Undoubtedly, many would die from the harsh conditions in the camps, but the fittest would survive, and they would have to be dealt with. Heydrich's subordinate, the infamous Adolf Eichmann, knew what that meant—extermination.

The method they devised became known as the death camp. There were several in Poland. The largest and most infamous of these was Auschwitz; others were Treblinka, Belzec, Sobibor, and Chelmno. Once the Jews or other "undesirables" such as Gypsies or homosexuals arrived, they would be examined carefully by SS men. Those who were healthy were assigned to the labor camps. The others—mainly the elderly and the children—were sent to the gas chambers.

Although they looked like shower rooms and were labeled "disinfection" chambers, these were actually cruel places of death, for instead of water, Zyklon-B, a pesticide gas, would flow out of the showerheads. The rooms were airtight, their doors sealed from the outside to prevent escape of the deadly gas—or the victims. After the victims were all dead, the Germans would collect the bodies, searching them closely for any remaining valuables, such as gold teeth.

This is a "disinfection" chamber at Auschwitz where the Nazis murdered Jews with Zyklon-B, a lethal gas.

Then the bodies would be burned in large ovens called crematoria. Sometimes the fat and ashes were used to make soap; other times, the skins of the victims were used to make leather goods.

In this way, the Nazis put some 4,000,000 Jews—of an estimated 5,700,000—to death. For those not sent immediately to the gas rooms, life was little better; they were forced into hard labor, fed just enough to keep from starving, and whipped and beaten constantly until they died or weakened so much that they were sent for "special" treatment.

This was Heydrich's plan and he carried it out with ruthless efficiency. He had always been every bit the committed anti-Semite that Hitler was; now, he became a mass murderer as well. But by the time he had laid the groundwork for the Final Solution, he had already taken on another job. This position gave him greater power and visibility than he had ever had, and, some felt, made him the man most likely to be named Hitler's successor: Reichsprotektor of Bohemia-Moravia.

6. Reichsprotektor

Heydrich's appointment as the head of occupied Czechoslovakia was the result of his and Himmler's plans to create an SS government for both Nazi Germany and its newly conquered territories. Himmler saw the SS eventually becoming more than just the elite of the Nazi organization; in time, the SS would dominate all aspects of life in Greater Germany. As a reward for helping wipe out the SA, Himmler had been allowed to create his own army, the *Waffen-SS* ("armed" SS), which eventually gained a reputation as fanatical fighters. But creating an army and running the secret police of the Third Reich were not enough to satisfy Himmler's and Heydrich's ambitions: They wanted to control the

In appreciation for his work with the SS, Hitler
appointed Heydrich head, or Reichsprotektor,
of Bohemia-Moravia, a German-occupied area
of Czechoslovakia.

occupied territories, to prove to Hitler what the SS could do if given total power over a region.

Heydrich, however, had to work hard to get his new position, as Himmler proved reluctant in the end to allow his most able subordinate to gain independence—both because he was grateful for his help and because he feared making Heydrich a rival. But Heydrich, working with his usual deviousness, had already taken steps to gain control of the protectorate.

The Czech Resistance Movement

The original protector of Bohemia-Moravia was Konstantin von Neurath, an aristocrat who had once been the German foreign minister. The protectorate had been set up with its own local government, which had to collaborate with the conquerors; von Neurath was content to allow these local leaders to do most of the work of running Bohemia-Moravia for him. Heydrich was able to exploit this fact by bombarding Himmler, and eventually Hitler, with reports about rising resistance to German rule.

There was, in fact, a Czech resistance movement, although Heydrich exaggerated its effectiveness. Edvard Benes, the exiled former president of Czechoslovakia, led the movement from Britain. After the fall of France in June of 1940, he was joined by the Czech Brigade, volunteers who had fled Czechoslovakia after the Nazis took over, in order to continue the struggle against Germany. Benes remained a popular figure in Czechoslovakia, and he worked to not only support the resistance there but to get the Allies to support the cause of Czechoslovakia, and not forget Hitler's first non-German victims.

Benes' methods included broadcasting to the people in Czechoslovakia and training the troops in the Czech Brigade for fighting in the future invasion of Europe by the Allies. He also pressed the British government to help supply the resistance in Czechoslovakia by dropping in supplies by plane. As the war progressed, he initiated a special training program for the best soldiers of the Czech Brigade, which taught them how to parachute from airplanes and gave them special training in sabotage and other areas that would be of aid to the resistance. The plan was to eventually drop these agents into Czechoslovakia to help strengthen the fight against the Nazis.

The problem Benes faced was that the Germans were well-known for being extremely brutal in crushing rebellions against their control. If the resistance worked too openly, or made life too difficult for the Germans, the ordinary Czech people would suffer cruelly at the hands of the Germans. Benes was well aware that only an invasion of Hitler's Europe could save Czechoslovakia. But soon he was forced to consider other methods.

Meanwhile, Heydrich's conspiracy against von Neurath was at last brought to a successful conclusion. Acts of sabotage against the German army—many likely committed by Heydrich's own agents—finally convinced Hitler that more drastic methods were required to subdue Bohemia-Moravia; von Neurath asked to be relieved for "health" reasons, and on September 21, 1941, Heydrich was appointed acting protector.

Heydrich had three major goals in taking over Bohemia-Moravia. He was concerned with the destruction of the resistance, increasing the productivity of the workers, especially those in the vital armaments factories, and, eventually, deciding who of the people of the former Czechoslovakia were fit to survive in the new Reich and who must be sent to be slaughtered.

Heydrich ordered a crackdown on the Czech resistance almost as soon as he took over. The Gestapo began rounding up dissidents and members of the resistance; thousands of arrests occurred in the first few months of Heydrich's rule alone. Many executions were ordered by the Nazi "special" courts because Heydrich very cleverly wanted

After the Sudetenland crisis, German forces invaded Czechoslovakia and crushed it completely.

the number of executions to appear to decline as time passed, creating the impression that he was restoring order. Many more people were undoubtedly killed in the concentration camps of Czechoslovakia and in Germany than Heydrich allowed to be reported.

The Czech resistance movement was thoroughly exposed and rooted out by the Gestapo, its patriotic members killed or sent to concentration camps, nearly destroying the entire operation. Benes, in England, lost communication with Czechoslovakia when the Germans destroyed the radio transmitters used by the resistance. Worse, they found and arrested his most important asset, a German officer code-named A-54, who had been giving the Czechs (and, through them, the Allies) reliable information about the plans of the German high command for several years.

A-54 was a man named Paul Thümmel, who was a member of the *Abwehr*, the German military intelligence agency, which was headed by Admiral Wilhelm Canaris, once a good friend of Heydrich but now secretly opposed not only to him but to Hitler and the war, as well. The Gestapo discovered Thümmel's work for the Allies, and he was arrested in March 1942. (The SS eventually killed him in prison in 1945, just a few days before the end of the war.)

Heydrich, however, wanted to do more than crush resistance to German rule; he also wanted the Czechs to work harder for the

Germans, and to eventually come to terms with being occupied by their neighbor. He therefore began a policy of giving better treatment to the workers in return for their loyalty. He increased their food rations, gave them unemployment and retirement benefits, and even gave some workers free holidays in luxury hotels. At the same time, however, he increased the amount of hours they had to work per week and ordered people in "non-essential" jobs to go to work in the armaments factory. He also cracked down on people who hoarded supplies or traded on the black market, although to create the impression that he was being "fair," Germans were executed for these crimes as well as Czechs.

The "Butcher of Prague"

The third part of Heydrich's plan was carried out with the same ruthless efficiency as the first two. In the SS vision of Greater Germany, there were only two classes of people: those who were racially fit to be "Germanized," and those who were racially inferior and had to be destroyed. This second category, of course, included the Jews, who were rounded up by the Gestapo and deported to Poland. Over 93,000 Jews were sent to the camps in Poland; just over 3,000 of them lived through the war.

As for the rest of the Czech population, Heydrich estimated that between 40 and 60

Czechoslovakian Jews were expelled from their homes and sent to Poland, where they were gassed.

percent of them would eventually have to be eliminated. To determine who should be Germanized and who murdered, Heydrich ordered a survey of the entire population of Bohemia-Moravia, under the guise of an examination for tuberculosis. Those found unfit would be sent, after the war, to the death camps in Poland. As for the children of Czechoslovakia, those who were "Aryan" enough would be sent to Germany, to be educated in Nazi schools; the rest would be slaughtered.

Heydrich's methods met with the approval of the Nazi leaders. He had crushed the Czech resistance, increased the productivity of the captured armaments factories, and apparently was well on his way to establishing a racially pure SS state that would one day become an integral part of the new Germany. However, Heydrich's extreme methods prodded the Allies into extreme action that would result in the end of the career of the "Butcher of Prague."

The actions of Heydrich in Czechoslovakia had already disturbed Benes; he decided that

Heydrich must be assassinated, an operation that was code-named "Anthropoid."

A View to a Kill

After combing through the members of the Czech Brigade being trained for parachute missions, two men were eventually selected: Josef Gabcik and Jan Kubis. These men, kept separate from the other trainees, realized that they were being prepared for a special mission.

The two men, who had both served in the Czech army, were to operate in total secrecy. Knowing how easily they could be discovered by the Gestapo, they were not even to tell other members of the Czech resistance about their job. Both men understood that they had little chance of surviving the mission.

After several agonizing delays while they waited for both the weather to be right and the British to have a plane available, Gabcik and Kubis finally parachuted into

Jan Kubis, one of Reinhard Heydrich's assassins, is pictured during his Czech resistance training.

Czechoslovakia on the night of December 28–29, 1941.

From the beginning, things went wrong. The agents were dropped off-target, some twenty miles from Prague, and Gabcik injured his foot while landing. Luckily, they were aided by people in the area who were sympathetic to the Czech resistance. Although it was against their orders, the two men were fortunate to have the help of the remnants of this organization, who gave them vital assistance in their plan to kill Heydrich.

The next few months were torture for Benes, who had very little contact with his agents. They had hoped to strike almost immediately, but had no opportunity to do so. However, they had two things in their favor: First, the resistance was in contact with servants who worked in Heydrich's palace and could give details of the Reichsprotektor's usual activities; and second, Heydrich's own lack of concern for his personal safety. He often traveled without a bodyguard, apparently feeling that he had to demonstrate that he had no fear of the Czechs; or perhaps it was just one last thrill after a lifetime of deliberately putting himself in danger, as he had when he was a fighter pilot. Whatever the reasons, his reckless disregard for his safety gave the two agents their chance to attack.

However, as spring and then summer approached, they still had not found a way to attack their target. Meanwhile, Heydrich was again plotting to gain more power within the Third Reich. He had been for a visit to occupied France, where he had helped strengthen the Gestapo activities, and there were rumors that he might soon be placed in charge of all of France. A meeting between Heydrich and Hitler was scheduled for May 27, 1942, where it was possible that he might be given this responsibility. The night before he was to leave, Heydrich went to a concert of his father's music. This was to be his last public appearance. The agents had found out he was leaving Czechoslovakia, possibly permanently, and had made the decision to strike.

Heydrich's Last Hours

The assassins selected a place in a suburb of Prague where the road made a sharp bend, which would force Heydrich's car to slow down. Shortly after 10:30 AM on May 27, 1942, as the Mercedes carrying the Reichsprotektor went by, Gabcik stepped up to the car, aiming his British-made Sten submachine gun. Unfortunately, the gun jammed when he pulled the trigger. Heydrich, shocked, stood up in the car, drew his pistol and yelled to his driver to stop. At that moment, Kubis stepped out of the shadows and threw a bomb at the car. It went off just below the rear wheel.

Heydrich and his driver jumped out of the wrecked car with their guns drawn, ready to fight their attackers, who fled into the crowd. But Heydrich had been hurt far more seriously than he thought, and soon collapsed. Fragments of his car's seat had been lodged in his body by the bomb blast, damaging his spleen and rupturing his diaphragm. He was rushed to a local hospital where emergency surgery was performed once a suitable Nazi doctor could be flown in from Germany, but infection set in. On June 4, 1942, Reinhard Heydrich, the perfect SS man, died.

The Perfect Nazi is Avenged

His death did not go unavenged. In retaliation, the small village of Lidice in Czechoslovakia was completely wiped out, the men shot by the SS, the women sent to concentration camps, along with those children not worthy of "Germanization." The entire village was then burned. Hitler, enraged by the assassination, wanted to arrest 10,000 Czechs and kill all the prisoners the Gestapo already had. Luckily for the Czechs, this terror was avoided, but for years they lived under extreme repression, as the SS and the Gestapo ruthlessly hounded the people.

The two assassins and several other members of the resistance hid out in the catacombs beneath a Greek Orthodox church in Prague. The Nazis, unable to find them, offered a huge reward for anyone who gave information about the whereabouts of the men. Karel Curda, a former sergeant in the Czech army and one of the agents parachuted into Czechoslovakia by Benes, eventually turned traitor and took the German money in exchange for telling the SS the location of the assassins. The SS attacked the church. After a desperate battle that lasted several hours, the resistance agents, including Gabcik and Kubis, shot themselves rather than face torture at the hands of the Gestapo.

Curda ended up marrying the sister of an SS officer and became a spy for the Gestapo. He was arrested after the war and hung by the Czechs as a traitor.

The Germans continued their reprisals against all the peoples of Europe. The systematic rounding up of Jews from eastern Europe in the following years was called "Operation Reinhard"—named after the man who had done so much to visit sorrow on the Jews of Europe. In a very real sense, the ghost of Reinhard Heydrich haunted Europe,

Heinrich Himmler (at far left) stands at attention as Heydrich's casket is brought out to be interred.

bringing unimaginable suffering to millions of people until the final collapse of Nazi Germany, which came almost three years after his death and the death of millions more of his victims.

Timeline

1931	Heydrich joins the Nazi Party.
1933	Adolf Hitler appointed German chancellor (prime minister) of Germany. The first concentration camp opens at Dachau. The first laws are passed to restrict Jewish rights. Berlin's Reichstag building is burned by the Nazis.
1934	Himmler and Heydrich initiate the "Night of the Long Knives" in Germany. The SS gains power and joins forces with Göring's Gestapo (secret state police).
1935	The Nuremberg Laws are passed, stripping Jews of their citizenry and forbidding marriages between Jews and non-Jews.
1936	Berlin hosts the Olympic Games. Heydrich spreads propaganda, hiding

the true face of Nazi Germany from the world.

1938

Himmler and Heydrich help Hitler gain power over Germany's War Ministry. *Kristallnacht* (the "Night of Broken Glass") occurs. German mobs destroy Jewish shops and synagogues.

1939

German forces enter the city of Prague, Czechoslovakia and eventually seize the nation, dividing it in two: the Protectorate of Bohemia-Moravia, run by the Third Reich and Slovakia, a Nazi "puppet" state. Germany invades Poland in September, beginning World War II. Britain, France, Australia, and New Zealand declare war on Germany. The concentration camp in Auschwitz opens. Heydrich is named Reichsprotektor (prime minister) of Bohemia-Moravia. Heydrich continues his plan to create two classes of people: those who are fit to be "Germanized," and those who are racially inferior and must be destroyed.

1940

Germany invades Norway and Heydrich begins assisting Hitler in his plan to conquer France. France surrenders in June. Mass deportation of Jews to concentration camps begins. Exiled former President of Czechoslovakia Edvard Benes leads the Czech resistance movement and plans to assassinate Heydrich in an operation code-named "Anthropoid."

1941
Hitler plans "Operation Barbarossa" and invades the Soviet Union, advancing toward Moscow.

1942
Wannsee Conference is held in January to address the "Jewish problem." Heydrich suggests the Final Solution, the extermination of the Jewish people. Together, the Nazis devise the death camp. Heydrich dies from wounds inflicted when assassins bomb his vehicle in a suburb of the city of Prague.

1944
Allied forces invade Normandy, France.

1945
Russians capture Auschwitz in February; American troops capture Buchenwald and Bergen-Belsen concentration camps in April. Germany surrenders in May.

Glossary

Allies
In World War II, Great Britain, France, the Soviet Union, and, after 1941, the United States.

Anschluss
German for "unification"; refers to the unification of Austria and Germany that was specifically forbidden by the Treaty of Versailles.

Auschwitz
Largest and most infamous of the German extermination camps in Poland; located near the town of Oswiecim in central Poland.

blitzkrieg
German for "lightning war"; refers to the combined air and tank attacks perfected by the Germans during World War II.

Einsatzkommando
"Special Action Commandos"; killing squads organized by the SS to exterminate Jews in the conquered regions of eastern Europe.

field marshall
The highest rank in most European armies, above a full general.

Final Solution
The Nazi plan to exterminate the Jews of Europe.

Führer
German word for "leader"; Hitler's title while he was dictator of Germany.

general government
Nazi "puppet" government set up in central Poland between the sections added directly to Germany and the parts occupied by the Soviet Union.

Gestapo
The *Geheime Staatspolizei,* or Secret State Police; the branch of the SS responsible for undercover espionage against enemies of the Nazis.

Kristallnacht
The "Night of Broken Glass," November 9, 1938, when the Nazis rampaged throughout Germany, destroying Jewish businesses and synagogues.

Luftwaffe
The German air force in World War II.

National Socialism (Nazism)
The theories of the Nazi Party as dictated by
Adolf Hitler.

NSDAP
The German initials for the National Socialist
German Worker's Party, the official name of the
Nazi Party.

SA
The *Sturmabteilung*, stormtroopers or
Brownshirts, a collection of thugs and criminals
that were the original enforcement branch of
the Nazi Party until replaced by the SS.

SD
The *Sicherheitsdienst*, the secret police division of
the SS.

SS
The *Schutzstaffel*, the black-uniformed elite of the
Nazi Party that controlled the Gestapo and ran
the concentration and extermination camps.

Treaty of Versailles
Treaty, or agreement, that ended World War I and
imposed harsh terms on Germany.

For More Information

American-Israeli Cooperative Enterprise (AICE)
2810 Blaine Drive
Chevy Chase, MD 20815
(301) 565-3918
Web site: http://www.us-israel.org

History Place
Web site: http://www.historyplace.com

Holocaust Education Foundation
P.O. Box 6153
Newport News, VA 23606-6153
E-mail: info@holocaust-trc.org
Web site: http://www.holocaust-trc.org

Simon Wiesenthal Center and Museum
    of Tolerance
1399 South Roxbury Drive
Los Angeles, CA 90035
(800) 900-9036

(310) 553-9036
E-mail: information@wiesenthal.net
Web site: http://www.wiesenthal.com

Survivors of the Shoah Visual History Foundation
P.O. Box 3168
Los Angeles, CA 90078-3168
(818) 777-4673
Web site: http://www.vhf.org

United States Holocaust Memorial Museum
100 Raoul Wallenberg Place SW
Washington, DC 20024-2126
(202) 488-0400
Web site: http://www.ushmm.org

For Further Reading

Adler, David A. *We Remember the Holocaust.* New York: Henry Holt, 1989.

Altshuler, David A. *Hitler's War Against the Jews.* New York: Behrman House, 1978.

Ayer, Eleanor. *The United States Holocaust Memorial Museum: America Keeps the Memory Alive.* New York: Dillon Press, 1994.

Chaikin, Miriam. *A Nightmare in History: The Holocaust 1933–45.* New York: Clarion Books, 1987.

Fox, Anne L., and Eva Abraham-Podietz, eds. *Ten Thousand Children: True Stories Told By Children Who Escaped the Holocaust on the Kindertransport.* West Orange, NJ: Behrman House, 1999.

Frank, Anne. *Diary of a Young Girl: The Definitive Edition.* New York: Doubleday, 1995.

Kallen, Stuart A. *The Nazis Seize Power, 1933–41.* Edina, MN: Abdo Publishing Co., 1994.

MacDonald, Callum. *The Killing of Reinhard Heydrich: The SS "Butcher of Prague."* New York: Da Capo Press, 1998.

Rice, Earle Jr. *Nazi War Criminals.* San Diego, CA: Lucent Books, 1998.

Rochman, Hazel, and Darlene Z. McCampbell, eds. *Bearing Witness: Stories of the Holocaust.* New York: Orchard Books, 1995.

Wiesel, Elie. *Night.* New York: Bantam Books, 1982.

For Advanced Readers

Calic, Edouard. *Reinhard Heydrich: The Chilling Story of the Man Who Masterminded the Nazi Death Camps.* New York: Morrow, 1985.

Gilbert, Martin. *The Holocaust: A History of Jews in Europe During the Second World War.* New York: Henry Holt & Co., 1985.

Knapp, Ron. *American Generals of World War II.* Springfield, NJ: Enslow Publishers, 1998.

Rogasky, Barbara. *Smoke and Ashes: The Story of the Holocaust,* rev. ed. New York: Holiday House, Inc., 2001.

Shirer, William L. *The Rise and Fall of the Third Reich: A History of Nazi Germany.* New York: Simon & Schuster, Inc., 1990.

Spiegelman, Art. *Maus: A Survivor's Tale: My Father Bleeds History.* New York: Pantheon Books, 1986.

Spiegelman, Art. *Maus II: A Survivor's Tale: And Here My Troubles Began.* New York: Pantheon Books, 1991.

Index

Credits

About the Author

Fred Ramen is a writer and computer programmer who lives in New York City.

Photo Credits

Layout

Nelson Sa